Mahatma Gandhi
and His Myths

Civil Disobedience, Nonviolence, and Satyagraha in the Real World

(Plus Why It's "Gandhi," Not "Ghandi")

Mark Shepard

Simple Productions
Friday Harbor, Washington
2011

Author Online!

For more resources, visit
Mark Shepard's Peace Page at

www.markshep.com/peace

ISBN-13: 978-0-938497-19-6
ISBN-10: 0-938497-19-7

Library of Congress subject headings:
Gandhi, Mahatma, 1869-1948—Political and social views
Nonviolence
Social change

This book was first published by Simple Productions, Arcata, California, 1990. This edition was first published by Shepard Publications, Los Angeles, 2002.

Version 2.2

I have been known as a crank, faddist, madman. Evidently the reputation is well deserved. For, wherever I go, I draw to myself cranks, faddists, and madmen.

Mahatma Gandhi

This is the text of the 1990 Annual Gandhi Lecture for the International Association of Gandhian Studies, delivered at the University of Virginia at Charlottesville on October 2.

THERE ARE MANY MYTHS ABOUT GANDHI. I'D like to point out a few of them and hopefully get rid of them for you.

First, a quick one: Gandhi was not a scrawny little man. Yes, his legs were scrawny—and bowed—but he had a barrel chest, and a deep, booming voice to match it. In pictures, you just don't notice his chest, because he usually had a cloth draped around it.

That was an easy one. Let's try another.

One of the most common and most dangerous myths about Gandhi is that he was a saint. The name—or rather, the title—*Mahatma* itself means "Great Soul." That's somewhere between a saint and a Messiah. Gandhi tried to avoid the title, but the people of India ignored his protests. Now I see that even the Library of Congress has begun to classify him under "Gandhi, Mahatma," so I guess he's lost *that* battle.

I've heard it argued that Gandhi indeed was a saint, since he was a master of meditation. Well, I must tell you that in all my readings of and about Gandhi, I've never come across anything to say that Gandhi was a master of meditation, or that he meditated at all—aside from observing a minute of silence at the beginning of his prayer meetings, a practice he said he borrowed from the Quakers.

Gandhi objected when people called him "a saint trying to be a politician." He said he was instead "a politician trying to be a saint." Personally, I go along with Gandhi's judgment on this.

Not that Gandhi's spiritual efforts and achievements shouldn't be honored. They've certainly inspired me. But if we label Gandhi a perfected being, we lose our chance to view his life and career critically and to learn from his mistakes.

Besides, if people see Gandhi as a saint, they'll think he's "too good for the world," and they won't take his example seriously as a model for concrete social change. I'm constantly annoyed at finding books on Gandhi in bookstore sections marked "Religious," or even "Occult." If his books are stashed away like that, how will the hard-boiled political scientists ever run across him?

* * *

Another myth about Gandhi is the idea that India's political leaders, beginning with Nehru, are the inheritors of his tradition and have carried it on.

I wish they had. But really, India's leaders have rejected much more of Gandhi than they've adopted.

They abandoned nonviolent action as soon as they attained power. India now sports the world's fourth largest armed force, and the leaders haven't seemed at all reluctant to use it to settle conflicts, either inside or outside the country. No thought is given to possible Gandhi-style alternatives.

Maybe even worse, India's leaders have done their best to imitate Western countries by building an economy based on large-scale industry and large-scale agriculture.

Gandhi fought this kind of development. He warned that it would economically ruin

India's villages, where 80% of India's people lived and *still* live. And Gandhi has proved correct.

Yes, India is now overall a much richer country—but it has more desperately poor people than ever. As many as half of its people can't afford enough food to sustain health. India prides itself now on growing enough grain so it doesn't need to import any—but the surplus rots in storage while people starve who can't afford to buy it!

Gandhi promoted a different kind of development. He stressed efforts based right in the villages, building on the villagers' own strengths and resources. Not many people here realize it, but Gandhi may be this century's greatest advocate of decentralism—basing economic and political power at the local level.

You may remember in the movie *Gandhi* seeing Gandhi spin cotton yarn on a compact spinning wheel. Gandhi and his colleagues were the ones who developed this wheel and introduced it into the villages. It's the first case of what's now called "appropriate technology" or "intermediate technology." Of course, E. F. Schumacher, the author of *Small is Beautiful,* later introduced the terms themselves. Schumacher was strongly influenced by Gandhi, calling him "the most important economic teacher today."

Gandhi set up a number of organizations to help carry out village development. He sent many workers to live in and among the villages.

Since his death, thousands have carried on this work. Now, though, the workers often combine development with campaigns against local injustice. Probably the closest thing in the United States to what they are doing is what we call "community organizing."

The people carrying on this work in India are among the true successors of Gandhi. Other modern-day Gandhians are in programs like the Chipko—"Hug the Trees"—Movement, which blocks irresponsible logging in the Himalayas; or Shanti Sena, the "Peace Army," which intervenes nonviolently in urban riots. My book *Gandhi Today* describes a number of the Gandhians' programs.

By the way, here's a quick bust of another myth concerning Gandhi and India's leaders: Indira Gandhi and her son Rajiv, the current prime minister, are no relation to the Mahatma. Indira Gandhi was the daughter of Nehru. The name "Gandhi" is common in India, and came to her by marriage. The name means "grocer."

* * *

I suspect, though, that most of the myths and misconceptions surrounding Gandhi have to do with nonviolence. For instance, it's surprising how many people still have the idea that nonviolent action is passive.

It's important for us to be clear about this: There is nothing passive about Gandhian nonviolent action.

I'm afraid Gandhi himself helped create this confusion by referring to his method at first as "passive resistance," because it was in some ways like techniques bearing that label. But he soon changed his mind and rejected the term.

Gandhi's nonviolent action was not an evasive strategy nor a defensive one. Gandhi was always on the offensive. He believed in confronting his opponents aggressively, in such a way that they could not avoid dealing with him.

But wasn't Gandhi's nonviolent action designed to avoid violence? Yes and no. Gandhi steadfastly avoided violence *toward his opponents.* He did not avoid violence toward himself or his followers.

Gandhi said that the nonviolent activist, like any soldier, had to be ready to die for the cause. And in fact, during India's struggle for independence, hundreds of Indians were killed by the British.

The difference was that the nonviolent activist, while willing to die, was never willing to kill.

Gandhi pointed out three possible responses to oppression and injustice. One he described as the coward's way: to accept the wrong or run away from it. The second option was to stand and fight by force of arms. Gandhi said this was *better* than acceptance or running away.

But the *third* way, he said, was best of all and required the most courage: to stand and fight solely by nonviolent means.

* * *

Another of the biggest myths about nonviolent action is the idea that Gandhi *invented* it.

Gandhi is often called "the father of non-violence." Well, he did raise nonviolent action to a level never before achieved. Still, it wasn't at all his invention.

Gene Sharp of Harvard University, in his book *Gandhi as a Political Strategist,* shows that Gandhi and his Indian colleagues in South Africa were well aware of other nonviolent struggles before they adopted such methods themselves. That was in 1906. In the couple of years before that, they'd been impressed by mass nonviolent actions in India, China, Russia, and among blacks in South Africa itself.

In another of his books, *The Politics of Nonviolent Action,* Gene Sharp cites over 200 cases of mass nonviolent struggle throughout history. And he assures us that many more will be found if historians take the trouble to look.

Curiously, some of the best earlier examples come from right here in the United States, in the years leading up to the American Revolution. To oppose British rule, the colonists used many tactics amazingly like Gandhi's—and according to Sharp, they used these techniques with more skill and sophistication than anyone else before the time of Gandhi.

For instance, to resist the British Stamp Act, the colonists widely refused to pay for the official stamp required to appear on publications and legal documents—a case of civil disobedience and tax refusal, both used later by Gandhi. Boycotts of British imports were organized to protest the Stamp Act, the Townshend Acts, and the so-called Intolerable Acts. The campaign against the latter was organized by the First Continental Congress, which was really a nonviolent action organization.

Almost two centuries later, a boycott of British imports played a pivotal role in Gandhi's own struggle against colonial rule.

The colonists used another strategy later adopted by Gandhi—setting up parallel institutions to take over functions of government—and had far greater success with it than Gandhi ever did. In fact, according to Sharp, colonial organizations had largely taken over control from the British in most of the colonies *before* a shot was fired.

* * *

Why aren't we more aware of such cases—including those in our own history? I think it's because of something we could call "filtering."

Probably most of you who've worked with cameras know about the kind of filter I mean. The filter fits over the camera lens and blocks out portions of the light—usually certain colors—and lets the remainder pass through to the lens. In effect, the filter selects the portion of light that the camera will "see."

Each of us too sees the world through our own "filter"—a filter made up of our assumptions, our motivations, and the categories we use to sort out and organize our experience. This filter determines how we see the world.

When we come across something that doesn't match our assumptions, motivations, and categories, our filter blocks it out. It's not that we choose to *reject* it. Consciously, we don't even *perceive* it. Or else we perceive it in a partial, distorted form.

It seems that nonviolence has a particularly hard time passing through many people's filters.

To know about current and past events, we depend a great deal on journalists and historians. Now, one thing that journalists and historians understand is military power. They know what comes from many people being shot or imprisoned. It's obvious when such power is being used, and a journalist or historian can feel professionally safe in describing and analyzing it.

But most of them do not deal so well with subtle, *nonviolent* forms of power. They don't understand how such power operates; or even how it *could* operate; or even that such a form of power could exist.

So, as often as not, they don't notice it at all. Or if they *do* notice it, they don't grasp what they've seen. Or they don't connect it with its effects.

For example, say that a Third World country undergoes a spontaneous, country-wide, mass noncooperation campaign against its dictator, lasting weeks or even months. Tens of thousands march in the streets, news-papers and radio stations defy the censors, whole cities are shut down for days at a time as people go on strike. Noted citizens call for the dictator's resignation, no one follows his orders, he has completely lost control.

Finally, four or five military officers, carrying out the obvious will of the people, march nearly unopposed into the presidential palace, arrest the dictator, and escort him out of office.

Chances are that our news media and history books will thereafter attribute the dictator's downfall, purely and simply, to "a military coup."

Watch the media closely, and you will find this is not at all an uncommon pattern. One classic example is in regard to the 1963 overthrow of South Vietnamese President Ngo Dinh Diem. An almost anti-climactic military coup followed a half year of intensive public actions led by Buddhist monks, in a campaign that destroyed Diem's base of support. Yet all three of the almanacs on my shelves ascribe Diem's downfall to the coup, and only one even mentions the popular campaign as a factor.

(By the way, for details on that popular movement, I refer you to what is probably the best overview of the worldwide nonviolence movement, *The Struggle for Humanity,* by Marjorie Hope and James Young.)

The fact is, even in revolutions that are primarily violent, the successful ones usually include nonviolent civilian actions not so different from the ones Gandhi used. And nearly every time, you will find these actions curiously downplayed or ignored by most journalists and historians.

As Indira Gandhi put it, "The meek may one day inherit the earth, but not the headlines."

* * *

So, Gandhi was definitely not "the father of nonviolence" in the sense of having invented it. But we might still grant him the title in something of the sense in which we say Isaac Newton "discovered" gravity.

Isaac Newton, of course, was not the first person to see an apple fall out of a tree. But Newton was the first person to notice that fall and grasp its significance, and provide *us* with a general concept so that we could do the same.

Newton, in other words, altered our filters so we could perceive the working of gravity.

The same with Gandhi. He seems to have been the first person to have the general *concept* of nonviolent action, to declare it, and then to consciously apply it on a large scale. In this way, he gave us all a way to perceive what he was up to.

Of course, some people still didn't get the point, because even when Gandhi laid it out for them, the concept of nonviolent action couldn't begin to pass through their clouded filters.

It's fun to read what's been written about Gandhi by his political opponents in England, or by Marxists in India and elsewhere, or by recent slanderers nipping at the heels of the movie *Gandhi.* What they've written doesn't reveal much about Gandhi, but it reveals a good deal about the writers.

Gandhi's most bitter critics have called him a charlatan—a deceiving, malicious fraud. After all, who could say the things Gandhi said and really mean them? Well, surely these critics couldn't!

Other, "kinder" critics have felt Gandhi was simply an idealistic fool, with no conception of how power works in the real world. Translated, this means that these critics can't understand how Gandhi's methods worked.

Let's look at these methods of Gandhi's and see if we can spot where their power might come from. And maybe we can clear up some other myths along the way.

* * *

Gandhi called his overall method of nonviolent action *Satyagraha.* This translates roughly as "Truth-force." A fuller rendering, though, would be "the force that is generated through adherence to Truth."

Nowadays, it's usually called *nonviolence.* But for Gandhi, *nonviolence* was the word for a different, broader concept—namely, "a way of life based on love and compassion." In Gandhi's terminology, Satyagraha—Truth-force—was an *outgrowth* of nonviolence.

It may also help to keep in mind that the terms *Satyagraha* and *nonviolent action,* though often used one for the other, don't actually refer to the exact same thing. Satyagraha is really one special *form* of nonviolent action—Gandhi's own version of it. Much of what's called nonviolent action wouldn't qualify as Satyagraha. But we'll come back to that later.

Gandhi practiced two types of Satyagraha in his mass campaigns. The first was *civil disobedience,* which entailed breaking a law and courting arrest. When we today hear this term, our minds tend to stress the "disobedience" part of it. But for Gandhi, "civil" was just as important. He used "civil" here not just in its meaning of "relating to citizenship and government" but also in its meaning of "civilized" or "polite." And that's exactly what Gandhi strove for.

We also tend to lay stress differently than Gandhi on the *phases* of civil disobedience. We tend to think breaking the law is the core of it. But to Gandhi, the core of it was going to prison. Breaking the law was mostly just a way to get there.

Now, why was that? Was Gandhi trying to fill the jails? Overwhelm and embarrass his captors? Make them "give in" through force of numbers?

Not at all. He just wanted to make a statement. He wanted to say, "I care so deeply about this matter that I'm willing to take on the legal penalties, to sit in this prison cell, to sacrifice my freedom, in order to show you how *deeply* I care. Because when you see the depth of my concern, and how 'civil' I am in going about this, you're bound to change your mind about me, to abandon your rigid, unjust position, and to let me help you see the truth of my cause."

In other words, Gandhi's method aimed to win not by overwhelming but by *converting* his opponent—or as the Gandhians say, by bringing about a "change of heart."

Now, to many people, that sounds pretty naive. Well, I'll let you in on a secret. It *was* naive. The belief that civil disobedience succeeded by converting the opponent happened to be a myth held by Gandhi himself. And it's shared by most of his admirers, who take his word for it without bothering to check it out.

As far as I can tell, no civil disobedience campaign of Gandhi's ever succeeded *chiefly* through a change of heart in his opponents.

But this doesn't mean civil disobedience didn't work. As a matter of fact, it *did* work. The only thing off-kilter was Gandhi's explanation of *how and why* it worked.

Let me give a general description of what seems really to have happened when Gandhi and his followers committed civil disobedience:

Gandhi and followers break a law—politely. Public leader has them arrested, tried, put in prison. Gandhi and followers cheerfully accept it all. Members of the public are impressed by the protest, public sympathy is aroused for the protesters and their cause.

Members of the public put pressure on public leader to negotiate with Gandhi. As cycles of civil disobedience recur, public pressure grows stronger. Finally, public leader gives in to pressure from his constituency, negotiates with Gandhi.

That's the general outline. Notice that there *is* a "change of heart," but it's more in the public than in the opponent. And notice too that there's an element of coercion, though it's indirect, coming from the public, rather than directly from Gandhi's camp.

Some campaigns of Gandhi's show a variation on this model. Sometimes Gandhi's opponents had superiors who wound up pressuring them or even ordering them to negotiate with Gandhi. These superiors might have been influenced by Gandhi's campaign, or by pressure from their *own* public—for instance, when British citizens pressured government leaders in Britain to intervene in affairs of their colonial government in India.

But the basic principle was the same: Gandhi's most decisive influence on his opponents was more indirect than direct.

Gandhi set out a number of rules for the practice of civil disobedience. These rules often baffle his critics, and often even his admirers set them aside as nonessential. But once you understand that civil disobedience, for Gandhi, was aimed at working a change of heart—whether in the opponent *or* the public—then it's easy to make sense of them.

One rule was that only specific, unjust laws were to be broken. Civil disobedience didn't mean flouting all law.

In fact, Gandhi said that only people with a high regard for the law were qualified for civil disobedience. Only action by such people could convey the depth of their concern and win respect. No one thinks much of it when the law is broken by those who care nothing for it anyway.

Other rules: Gandhi ruled out direct coercion, such as trying to physically block someone. Hostile language was banned. Destroying property was forbidden. Not even secrecy was allowed.

All these were ruled out because any of them would undercut the empathy and trust

Gandhi was trying to build, and would hinder that "change of heart."

* * *

The second form of mass Satyagraha was *noncooperation.*

This is just what it sounds like. Noncooperation meant *refusing to cooperate* with the opponent, refusing to submit to the injustice being fought. It took such forms as strikes, economic boycotts, and tax refusals.

Of course, noncooperation and civil disobedience overlapped. Noncooperation too was to be carried out in a "civil" manner. Here too, Gandhi's followers had to cheerfully face beating, imprisonment, confiscation of their property—and it was hoped that this willing suffering would cause a "change of heart."

But noncooperation also had a dynamic of its own, a dynamic that didn't at all depend on converting the opponent or even molding public opinion. It was a dynamic based not on appeals but on the power of the people themselves.

Gandhi saw that the power of any tyrant depends entirely on people being willing to obey. The tyrant may *get* people to obey by threatening to throw them in prison, or by holding guns to their heads. But the power still resides in the obedience, not in the prison or the guns.

Now, what happens if those people begin to say, "We're not afraid of prison. We're even willing to die. But we're not willing to obey you any longer."

It's very simple. The tyrant has no power. He may rant and scream and hurt and destroy—but if the people hold to it, he's finished.

Gandhi said, "I believe that no government can exist for a single moment without the cooperation of the people, willing or forced, and if people suddenly withdraw their cooperation in every detail, the government will come to a standstill."

That was Gandhi's concept of power—the one he's accused of not having. It's a hard one to grasp, for those used to seeing power in the barrel of a gun. Their filters do not pass it. And so they call Gandhi idealistic, impractical.

* * *

Then there are the critics who say nonviolent action worked fine in India, but they don't think it would make sense to use it elsewhere. These critics believe that Indians are particularly suited to nonviolent action, because of the ethic of nonviolence built into their religion.

This is a very interesting myth, and those who believe in it certainly possess a very selective filter. Personally, I don't think you can follow the news from India for long and still believe Indians are less violent than other people.

Besides, Gandhi's philosophy of nonviolence seems to have been consciously inspired first by the New Testament—the Sermon on the Mount. Only later, it seems, did he find similar ideas in Hindu scriptures.

It's surprising how easy it is to forget that we too have an ethic of nonviolence built into our society's chief religion. We just don't happen to follow it. Just as the Indians don't normally follow theirs.

But really, the easiest way to see that nonviolent action is suitable outside India is simply to look at all the *cases* of nonviolent action outside India. Unless your filter is pretty murky, you can hardly miss them. It certainly can't be easy to ignore the example of Martin Luther King, Jr., or to forget the Solidarity movement in Poland, or to overlook the overthrow of Ferdinand Marcos in the Philippines.

Then there's the *cousin* of the "only-in-India" argument. This one says that nonviolent action can work only against "easy" enemies like the British, and not against, say, the Soviets, or Central American dictators, or those villains of last resort, the Nazis.

Here again, filters are in place, because nonviolent action has been used with *some* success against *all* these.

In 1968, Czechoslovakian civilians nonviolently held Soviet armed forces at bay for a full week and stopped the Soviet leaders from ever subjugating that country to the degree they had intended. In 1944, military dictators were ousted nonviolently in both El Salvador *and* Guatemala. And during World War II, Norway nonviolently and successfully resisted Nazi attempts to reorganize its society along fascist lines.

(In case you missed any of these, you can find details, again, in Gene Sharp's *The Politics of Nonviolent Action,* among other sources.)

One of the interesting things about the many instances of nonviolent struggle around the world is that, even today, it is often by people who know nothing or next to nothing about Gandhi. After you look at a number of these, you have to conclude that people in many situations just *naturally* turn to such methods.

On the other hand, if you look closely at so-called popular liberation movements, you'll find that they're seldom started by the peasants or workers they're supposed to benefit. These armed struggles may gradually build wider support—but in almost every case, they're launched by students or other intellectuals in the *name* of the people.

* * *

Still another group of Gandhi's critics says: Maybe nonviolent action does work—but it's just too slow. People are suffering injustice, slavery, starvation, murder. How can you ask them to be patient and work nonviolently?

Somehow people have developed the myth that nonviolent action is slow, while violence is quick. But I don't believe you can find evidence for this in history.

Now, I'm not going to try to prove my point by comparing cases of violent and nonviolent struggles. There are so many variables that comparisons from one situation to another really don't mean anything.

But we can still rid ourselves of the idea that violence is necessarily quick. If we look at the Chinese Revolution, for instance, we find that Mao Tse-Tung and his Communist forces were engaged in combat over a period of 22 years. Vietnam was embattled for an even longer period: 35 years. These are not swift victories.

We can also dispel the notion that nonviolent action has to be slow. The nonviolent overthrow of Marcos in the Philippines—

measured from the assassination of Benigno Aquino—took only three years.

Where does the idea come from, then, that violence is quick and nonviolence is slow? Well, violence *feels* quicker, because time passes rapidly when you're dodging bullets. Nonviolent action, on the other hand, requires more patience because the action is less thrilling.

Theodore Roszak once commented on the impatience of some of these critics. He said, "People try nonviolence for a week, and when it 'doesn't work,' they go back to violence, which hasn't worked for centuries."

Now, what does Roszak mean, that violence "hasn't worked for centuries"? Is he ignoring the success of so many violent revolutions? I think Roszak means that violence, even when it succeeds, has major negative side-effects—side-effects that nonviolent action mostly avoids.

First of all, a violent struggle will tend to bring about much more destruction of life, property, and environment.

Of course, there can be destruction in nonviolent struggles, too. Just because *you're* nonviolent doesn't mean your *opponent* will be. As I said before, Gandhi's campaigns in India saw hundreds of Indians killed by the British. Still, this doesn't compare with the tens or hundreds of thousands, or even millions, killed in some violent revolutions.

The difference, by the way, doesn't arise because nonviolent struggles are aimed at "nice" enemies. After all, the British aren't so much nicer than the French, who killed 800,000 Algerians—that's one out of every thirteen—during Algeria's war of independence.

No, the difference arises because, in a violent struggle, the violence of each side goads the other to *greater* violence. Also, each side uses the violence of the other side to *justify* its own violence. A nonviolent struggle, on the other hand, doesn't so much encourage the violence of the opponent.

Other negative side-effects of violence come into view once the struggle comes to an end. For instance, violence generally leaves the two sides as long-standing enemies.

Maybe the most amazing thing about Gandhi's nonviolent revolution is, not that the

British left, but that they left as friends, and that Britain and India became partners in the British Commonwealth.

Gandhi noted also that violent revolutions almost always end in repressive dictatorships. Once the rebel troops gain control, they naturally keep acting as they're used to—in other words, they start running the country like a military camp. And of course, there are lots of bitter enemies within the country who still need to be put down and kept down. Gandhi hoped that a nonviolent revolution, led by civilians, would avoid all this.

Now, India today is not a paradise. It is afflicted by widespread injustice, civil violence, and authoritarian trends. Still, it is one of the few Third World countries where democracy in any form has survived continuously. There has never been a military coup in India.

When you look at the side-effects of violent struggle, you really have to ask yourself, just who is being practical here, and who is not.

* * *

Now, maybe you think from all I've said that I believe nonviolent action would work anywhere, if people just gave it a try. Actually, I don't. I believe there are cases in which nonviolent action wouldn't stand a chance, and where any attempt at it is futile. In some of these cases, violence might succeed—in its own fashion.

On the other hand, the cases in which nonviolent action wouldn't work are often just the cases in which violence as well would prove pointless or worse.

The belief that violence will work wherever nonviolent action wouldn't is a very puzzling myth. The opposite case is likely more common: Where violent efforts would be easily contained or instantly crushed, nonviolent action may be the only realistic choice.

Then there are other cases, I believe, in which violence would work, but so would nonviolent action—with much less harm.

If exponents of armed struggle were less concerned with proving their manliness and more concerned with the welfare of the people they claim to stand up for, they might discover that nonviolent forms of struggle, everything considered, work better.

* * *

I'd like to bust one more myth about Gandhi's nonviolent action. This one is held both by many of Gandhi's critics and by many of his admirers. In fact, the misunderstanding is so common and so basic that I have to say that many—maybe most—admirers of Gandhi's methods really miss the point.

Just as *I* did when I began my study of Gandhi.

Prior to that study, most of my experience with political activism had been with Marxists, and I had pretty well absorbed their worldview. But later, after exploring several spiritual traditions, I felt I could no longer endorse the Marxists' methods.

How then to oppose injustice and reform society? I hoped that Gandhi held the answer. It seemed to me he had meant to work out just what I was looking for: a way of defeating and overthrowing the oppressors of the world, but by moral means.

That was *my* myth about Gandhi; that was my filter. I had to read an entire book and a half about Gandhi before it struck me—and it struck me hard—that Gandhi was not talking about defeating or overthrowing *anyone.*

Satyagraha—Gandhi's nonviolent action—was *not* a way for one group to seize what it wanted from another. It was *not* a weapon of class struggle, or of any other kind of division. Satyagraha was instead an instrument of *unity.* It was a way to remove injustice and restore social harmony, to the benefit of *both sides.*

Satyagraha, strange as it seems, was for the opponent's sake as well. When Satyagraha worked, *both sides won.*

That concept did not pass at all easily through my filter, and I understand why so many others miss it entirely. But it is, really, the essential difference between Gandhi's Satyagraha and so much of the nonviolent action practiced by others.

You may wonder, how did Gandhi himself come to this amazing attitude? He said it this way: "All my actions have their source in my inalienable love of humankind."

You see, love for the victim demanded struggle, while love for the opponent ruled out doing harm. But in fact, love for the opponent likewise demanded struggle.

Why? Because by hurting others, the oppressor also hurts himself.

Of course, the oppressor isn't likely to be aware of that. He may be thoroughly enjoying his power and wealth. But beneath all that, his injustice is cutting him off from his fellow humans and from his own deeper self. And when that happens, his spirit can only wither and deform.

Now, that's *not* obvious, and if you don't believe it, I don't know any way I might convince you.

But if that does pass through your filter, you may be well on your way to understanding Gandhi.

Author Online!

For more resources, visit
Mark Shepard's Peace Page at

www.markshep.com/peace

Bibliography

Mohandas K. Gandhi, *Nonviolent Resistance,* Schocken, New York, 1967. A collection of writings on nonviolence.

Marjorie Hope and James Young, *The Struggle for Humanity: Agents of Nonviolent Change in a Violent World,* Orbis, Maryknoll, New York, 1977. Portraits of important leaders and groups in the worldwide nonviolence movement.

Mark Shepard, *Gandhi Today,* Simple Productions, Arcata, California, and Seven Locks Press, Washington, D.C., 1987. On successors of Gandhi in India and around the world.

Gene Sharp, *Gandhi as a Political Strategist,* Porter Sargent, Boston, 1979. A collection of Sharp's articles on Gandhi and nonviolence.

———, *The Politics of Nonviolent Action,* Porter Sargent, Boston, 1973. An extensive look at methods and historical examples of nonviolence. The paperback edition is in three volumes.

A Note on the Name

Gandhi is spelled "Gandhi." G-a-n-d-h-i.

Half the time that you see this name in Western newspapers and magazines, it's spelled "Ghandi." As if *Gandhi* meant some sort of *ghoul.* It doesn't!

How can the *h* go after the *d* instead of the *g?* Because *dh* represents a single Indian consonant, the "aspirated" *d.* Yes, India also has an aspirated *g,* but it's not in *Gandhi*!

Here's a bonus question: At the end of a line, where can you break *Gandhi*? Not between the *d* and the *h*! The break is after the *n,* as in "Gan-dhi." *Dh* is a single consonant, remember?

You are now among the few Westerners who can spell *Gandhi.*

I hope.

Index

About the Author

Mark Shepard's writings on social alternatives have appeared in over thirty publications in the United States, Canada, England, Norway, Germany, the Netherlands, Switzerland, Japan, and India. The American Library Association *Booklist* called his book *Gandhi Today* "a masterpiece of committed reporting." Visit him at

www.markshep.com/peace

CPSIA information can be obtained at www.ICGtesting.com
Printed in the USA
LVOW10s1324150715

446342LV00002B/69/P

9 780938 497196